Massachusetts

A Buddy Book
by

Julie Murray

ABDO
Publishing Company

VISIT US AT

www.abdopub.com

Published by ABDO Publishing Company, 4940 Viking Drive, Edina, Minnesota 55435.

Printed in the United States.

Edited by: Sarah Tieck
Contributing Editor: Michael P. Goecke
Graphic Design: Deb Coldiron, Maria Hosley
Image Research: Sarah Tieck
Photographs: Clipart.com, Corbis, Getty Images, Library of Congress, North Wind Picture Archives, One Mile Up, Photodisc, Photos.com. Special thanks to the National Scenic Byways Program (www.byways.org) for use of the photo on page 15.

Library of Congress Cataloging-in-Publication Data

Murray, Julie, 1969-
Massachusetts / Julie Murray.
p. cm. — (The United States)
Includes bibliographical references and index.
ISBN 1-59197-680-4
1. Massachusetts—Juvenile literature. I. Title.

F64.3.M87 2005
974.4—dc22

2005040373

Table Of Contents

A Snapshot Of Massachusetts

When people think of Massachusetts, they think of history. It was one of the first states in the United States. Also, the Pilgrims landed in Massachusetts. Many important events during the American Revolutionary War happened there.

A view of Boston and
Massachusetts Bay.

There are 50 states in the United States.
Every state is different. Every state has an
official state nickname. Massachusetts is
known as the "Bay State." This is because
early settlers made their home on
Massachusetts Bay.

Many people live and work
in Massachusetts.

Massachusetts became the sixth state
on February 6, 1788.

Massachusetts has 8,262 square miles
(21,398 sq km). It is the 45th-largest state in
the United States. Massachusetts is home
to 6,349,097 people.

Where Is Massachusetts?

There are four parts of the United States. Each part is called a region. Each region is in a different area of the country. The United States Census Bureau says the four regions are the Northeast, the South, the Midwest, and the West.

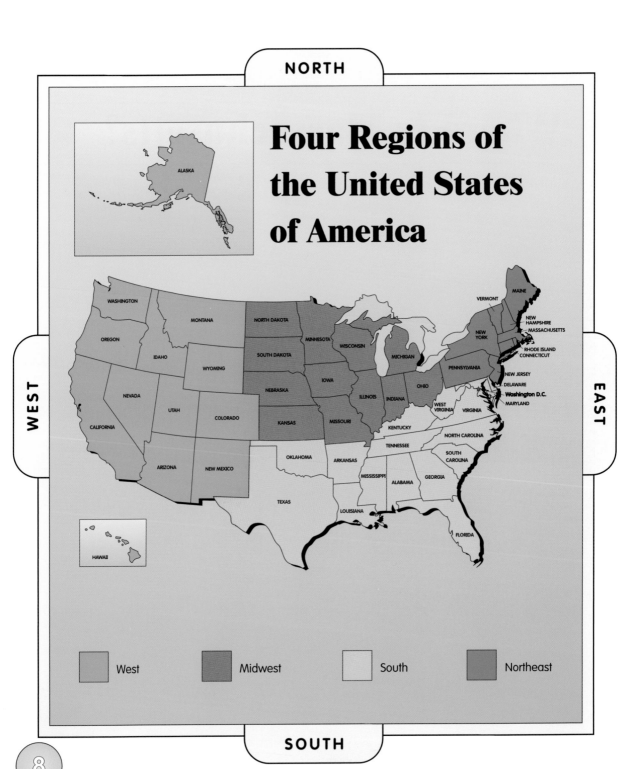

Four Regions of the United States of America

West   Midwest   South   Northeast

Massachusetts is located in the Northeast region. The weather in this part of the United States is cool. Sometimes it snows in Massachusetts. There have also been hurricanes in this state.

Massachusetts is cold in the winter. Sometimes it snows.

Massachusetts is bordered by five states and a body of water. New Hampshire and Vermont are to the north. New York lies to the west. Connecticut and Rhode Island are to the south. The Atlantic Ocean forms Massachusetts's eastern border.

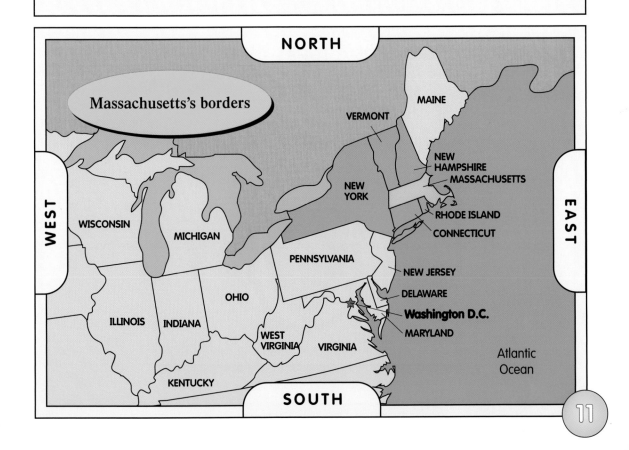

NORTH

WEST

EAST

SOUTH

Massachusetts's borders

MAINE

VERMONT

NEW HAMPSHIRE

MASSACHUSETTS

RHODE ISLAND

CONNECTICUT

NEW YORK

WISCONSIN

MICHIGAN

PENNSYLVANIA

NEW JERSEY

DELAWARE

OHIO

Washington D.C.

ILLINOIS

INDIANA

MARYLAND

WEST VIRGINIA

VIRGINIA

Atlantic Ocean

KENTUCKY

Massachusetts

State abbreviation: MA

State nickname: The Bay State

State capital: Boston

State motto: *Ense petit placidam sub libertate quietem* (Latin for "By the Sword We Seek Peace, but Peace Only Under Liberty")

Statehood: February 6, 1788, 6th state

Population: 6,349,097, ranks 13th

Land area: 8,262 square miles (21,398 sq km), ranks 45th

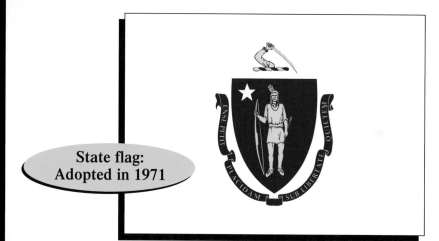

State flag:
Adopted in 1971

State tree: Live oak

State song: "All Hail to Massachusetts"

State government: Three branches: legislative, executive, and judicial

Average July temperature: 71°F (22°C)

Average January temperature: 25°F (-4°C)

State flower: Mayflower

State bird: Black-capped chickadee

State horse: Morgan horse

Cities And The Capital

Boston is the largest city in Massachusetts. It is also the state capital. Boston is famous for its history. It is where the Boston Tea Party happened. The Boston Tea Party was an important event in American history.

A view of the city of Boston.

Today, people reenact the Boston Tea Party.

Worcester is the second-largest city in the state. It is located about 40 miles (64 km) west of Boston.

Famous Citizens

John F. Kennedy (1917–1963)

John Fitzgerald Kennedy was born in 1917 in Brookline. He is famous for being the youngest elected president of the United States. He was only 43 years old when he became president. He was the 35th president of the United States. He was president from 1961 to

John F. Kennedy

1963. Kennedy was known for his work with other countries and with civil rights. He was shot and killed on November 22, 1963. This was a very tragic event in American history.

Famous Citizens

Benjamin Franklin (1706-1790)

Benjamin Franklin was born in 1706 in Boston. He had 16 brothers and sisters. He is famous for his many talents. He helped make the United States a country. Franklin signed the Declaration of Independence. He was an inventor, a writer, and a printer. He also helped to create the first city hospital in the United States.

Benjamin Franklin

The Pilgrims

Massachusetts is where the Pilgrims landed and set up the first permanent settlement in America. The Pilgrims were from England, a country in Europe. They sailed to America on a boat called the *Mayflower*. The Pilgrims arrived in America in 1620. They settled in Plymouth, Massachusetts. Back then, America was a great wilderness.

The first winter in America was hard.
The Pilgrims did not have enough food.
Many people died.

In the spring of 1621, the Pilgrims met some Native Americans. A Native American named Squanto helped the Pilgrims. He shared what he knew about fishing, hunting, and farming. The Native Americans gave the Pilgrims corn, beans, and squash to plant.

The Pilgrims carefully tended their crops. Their crops grew a lot of food. The Pilgrims were happy to have a good harvest. This meant that they would not run out of food.

The Pilgrims decided to celebrate their good harvest. They invited the Wampanoag Native Americans to a meal. People played games and told stories. This celebration is what many people call the "First Thanksgiving." It lasted for three days.

The first Thanksgiving was in Massachusetts.

Salem Witch Trials

Salem is famous for the Salem Witch Trials. These happened in 1692. More than 100 people from Salem and nearby towns were put on trial for witchcraft. This was a scary time in Massachusetts.

A witch trial in Salem.

The Salem Witch Trials started when a
few girls accused a woman of being a witch.
They said she tried to hurt them with magic.

Soon, many other townspeople were accused of practicing witchcraft. About 150 people were put in jail during this time. Many of these people were also put on trial. Twenty men and women died because people thought they were practicing witchcraft.

The Salem Witch Trials ended in 1693. Today, what happened in Salem is known as a "witch hunt."

During the Salem Witch Trials, hundreds of people were accused and jailed for practicing witchcraft.

Cape Cod

Cape Cod is a 65-mile (105-km) peninsula. It sticks out into the Atlantic Ocean. When people think of Cape Cod, they think of the seashore. The Cape Cod National Seashore has more than 43,000 acres (17,400 ha) of beaches, sand dunes, woodlands, and ponds.

Millions of people vacation at Cape Cod each summer. They hunt for seashells, hike, bike, and spend time in the Atlantic Ocean. Fresh seafood is available to eat. Cape Cod got its name because fishermen catch codfish in nearby waters.

A view of Cape Cod.

Massachusetts

1602: Bartholomew Gosnold arrives in Massachusetts.

1636: Harvard University is the first college in the colonies.

1773: On the night of December 16, people from the colony went aboard English ships. They dumped 342 chests filled with tea into Boston Harbor. They did this to protest the British government.

1788: Massachusetts becomes the sixth state on February 6.

1797: John Adams of Braintree becomes the second president of the United States.

1825: John Quincy Adams of Braintree becomes the sixth president of the United States.

1891: In Springfield, James Naismith invents the game of basketball.

1937: Ruth Wakefield invents the chocolate chip cookie at the Toll House Inn in Whitman.

1961: John F. Kennedy of Brookline becomes the 35th president of the United States.

1986: Boston Celtics win their record 16th NBA Championship.

2004: Boston Red Sox win the World Series for the first time since 1918.

The Boston Red Sox after their World Series win.

Cities in Massachusetts

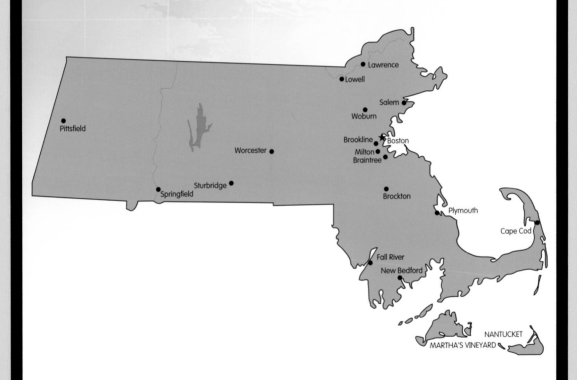

Lawrence
Lowell
Salem
Woburn
Pittsfield
Brookline
Boston
Worcester
Milton
Braintree
Sturbridge
Springfield
Brockton
Plymouth
Cape Cod
Fall River
New Bedford
NANTUCKET
MARTHA'S VINEYARD

Important Words

American Revolutionary War Americans fought for freedom from Great Britain in this famous war.

capital a city where government leaders meet.

civil rights rights for all citizens.

colony a settlement. Colonists are the people who live in a colony.

harvest what is gathered from ripe crops. A harvest may be vegetables, fruit, grains, and many other things.

hurricane a storm that forms over warm seawater with winds more than 74 miles (119 km) per hour.

nickname a name that describes something special about a person or a place.

peninsula a piece of land surrounded by water on three sides.

wilderness wild, unsettled land.

Web Sites

To learn more about Massachusetts, visit ABDO Publishing Company on the World Wide Web. Web site links about Massachusetts are featured on our Book Links page. These links are routinely monitored and updated to provide the most current information available.

www.abdopub.com

Index